Therapists' Ethics

Versus
Satin Susan

Richard Bennett

authorHOUSE®

AuthorHouse™
1663 Liberty Drive, Suite 200
Bloomington, IN 47403
www.authorhouse.com
Phone: 1-800-839-8640

First published by AuthorHouse 9/24/2008

ISBN: 978-1-4389-0553-2 : (sc)

Printed in the United States of America
Bloomington, Indiana

This book is printed on acid-free paper.

It takes courage to read
And understand this book.

Table of Contents

Prologue

Readers, particularly psychotherapists, will have to decide if this little book is real or fantasy. You also will have to decide if this is an x-rated story or not. This little book is intended to discuss one of the main themes found in the various professional codes of ethics. This is the story of three different therapists, a Christian counselor (social worker), a psychiatrist and a psychologist. It is also a love story, if you can find it.

Susan

My name is Susan. I am about 5'6" with a good body. I work out regularly, not for muscles but for tone. I have blue eyes and long brown hair. I almost always wear sexy satin panties from Victoria's Secret. Some people say that I look like the model on pages 26 and 27, of the fall, 2007 issue of Victoria's Secret Look Book, or page 84 of the 2007 winter Fingerhut catalogue. I like the no-show, bikini panty the best. And, of course, because I am financially endowed, I have had my own designers make me some very special, seductive, satin panties.

I'm often told I look 30, but I'm really 42.

I probably have a sexual problem.

Chapter One

It is early fall, the wind is blowing quite hard, and it is a bit chilly. I stand here briefly before I open the door. I choose my long skirt with the long slit up the front and my sheer blouse that I usually wear for these occasions. The wind picks up my skirt showing for a moment my satin panties. (I always wear satin panties.) My long flowing brown hair looks tussled and windblown now, after I worked so hard to get it just right, but I still look pretty good.

I have been to many therapists before. I particularly like the young ones just out of graduate school; they are so new, so naïve, so fresh and so stupid. They all receive the generic psychotherapeutic education available these days and have memorized but not internalized their Code of Ethics. They have not experienced the real world yet.

I AM THE REAL WORLD.

I open the smudged door and find myself in an eight by seven foot waiting room. There was an attempt at what I call "non-profit" style, but several very uncomfortable plastic chairs line three off-white, painted walls, which feature some tattered pictures that must have been purchased in the 1950s. A small table holds two-year-old magazines, placed so neatly and compulsively that I don't dare take one for fear of messing them up.

Another table in a corner appears to be a little altar with an empty cross and an open Bible. A faded picture of *Jesus at the Door Knocking,* hangs above the little corner alter.

The stiff, unsmiling receptionist quips, "What therapist are you looking for?"

I respond, "I think his name is Bill Jones."

She then asks me my name, and I respond, "Susan Mullins."

After checking the appointment book and the clock, she responds, "Yes, Dr. Jones is here and expects you. Would you please fill out these forms?"

When I look at the forms, they are almost reprints, much the same, as the ones used by the other therapists that I have been to. The forms include the necessary confidentiality statements and ask for my signature several times. There's insurance information, contact phone numbers, emergency phone numbers, my employment information, and some additional HIPPA Information, which shows that my government is still at work for me.

I explain to the receptionist, "I do not work. I will pay cash. There is no insurance and no employer."

She responds with a stiff, "Thank you. Please have a seat. Doctor, will be with you in about five minutes."

I pick out which of the plastic chairs will give me the best advantage for a first impression and decide on the green one.

I sit down. Ugh! I knew it—a flexi chair from Wal-Mart, and I have no place to put my long, cleanly shaven legs. So I stretch them out, and my skirt gently falls open revealing most of my legs and hinting at a bit of realistic and exciting sexuality.

As I sit here, I watch a couple come out of what must be the door to the hallway leading to the four therapists' offices. (I know there are four therapists, because their names are lined up on one of those black, framed punch boards, which use the white plastic letters, also from Wal-Mart.) The couple schedules an appointment for more marital counseling. While the wife makes the appointment, her husband turns and looks- really he stares at me-and almost comes in his pants. I simply smile back.

After the couple leaves, the receptionist stands up, and with a slight gesture of her hand directs me to enter the same door the couple came through, and she walks me down the hall to Dr. Jones' office. It's a small office just big enough for a very small family to squeeze in. Noticing more wobbly, plastic waiting room chairs stacked in the corner of his office, I gather Dr. Jones sees plenty of families in this cramped space called his office. The chair stack screams out that going to this therapist is hard and uncomfortable.

The same type of 1950 pictures, that hung in the waiting room, clutter Dr. Jones' off-white walls, caging in the two plastic wicker chairs, which seem a bit more comfortable than the waiting room chairs.

Dr. Jones is sitting behind a little IKEA student desk, facing the door; a typical office desk could not fit in his office. Another picture of Christ is hanging behind the desk, and I notice a small autographed picture of Jerry Faldwell sitting on his desk. Dr. Jones is thin, very young looking, about twenty-seven, wearing a very plain, non-descript blue suit. His tie, the ugliest green tie ever, does not coordinate with his suit or the multi-colored, flowery shirt which he is wearing. God, he looks like weeds growing in a topsy-turvy garden.

Hanging next to Christ are his certificates, one from an accredited school of social work, a doctorate degree from some school of divinity, totally unknown to me. There is another empty crucifix hanging on the wall, near the stack of chairs. I feel like I am in a pastor's study, and it's been a long time since I was in one of those, believe me.

Dr. Jones extends his boney hand and says, "Welcome," without standing up and motions me to a plastic wicker-looking chair, "Please sit down."

I sit down on another hard chair in the sexiest way that I can and make sure that most of my tanned long legs show, almost up to my hips.

"I always pray before each therapy session, will you join me?" he says. I nod, and he prays, "Dear God, let us do Thy will, and solve all the problems that this woman brings to Us and help us through Thy word both to know and understand Thy will, in the name of the Father, Son and Holy Ghost, A-men."

The Amen resonates in the small office, like it was spoken loudly in a large sanctuary. Maybe Dr. Jones has practiced it ten thousand times or maybe he really is a preacher.

I didn't pray with him; I don't pray. I looked around the room instead and found a picture, evidently of his wife. There are no pictures of children.

He begins with the usual questions, while his eyes fixate on my long tan legs. "Name, please."

"Susan Mullins, I live in a loft in the Old City, and my cell number is on the forms I filled out for your secretary earlier. He seems surprised that I am going to pay his $100 fee in cash, but it fits with the image that I was trying to portray, a wealthy, sexy lady. I am wealthy and I can be very sexy.

Next he asks, "Susan, what problems may I help you with?"

I respond, "I just don't feel right. My boyfriend of six years just left me, and I feel devastated. I tend to cry most of the time."

"That is understandable," he replies, "Have you thought of taking your loneliness to God and becoming a Christian?"

I ask what he means, and he very seriously says, "God can solve all your problems if you will just call upon Him."

Can I really talk about sex with God?

"I tried," I say, as I slowly unbutton the top button of my blouse, revealing my perfectly formed breasts to the nipples, "but nothing happened."

"We are never lonely with God," he responds. "He is with us always, and all we have to do is call upon Him."

"I've called and called, and I never get an answer. All I get is this emptiness in the pit of my stomach."

"What does that feel like?" Dr. Jones pries.

"What does what feel like?"

"What does your stomach feel like?" he continues, forcing an answer.

"Like shit! Like I'm so used to having a strong, mature partner lying next to me that now when I am alone my stomach feels hungry, starving, but I can't eat," I whine, looking very sad.

"Have you ever eaten from the Bread of Life?" he inquires.

I really have no clue what he means, so I ask.

Sometimes quoting from the Bible, Dr. Jones describes Jesus "as the Bread of Life," ending with, "he who believes on Him will have everlasting life."

"Can I sleep with Jesus?" I ask. "He was human, you know?"

Well, now that seems to offend Dr. Jones.

"Jesus is Holy and not sexual," he responds disgustedly, as his fascination with my legs and perfect breasts continues. "Sex out-of-wedlock is a sin, Susan."

I offer no response. Everything is quiet, as he fixates on my body, but I don't push it.

After a few moments, I break the silence, "I know that I am a sinner, I just can't stop having these dreams of a strong person, like you, Dr. Jones, laying next to me in my bed and holding me tight."

If it were proper to drool, he would be drooling, but then he mutters, "How many times have you sinned?"

"You mean had sex with Jesus or someone else?" I know I'm pushing his buttons.

"Yes," he says, while appearing very perturbed.

"Many" I respond, and now changing the intensity of the moment, "I am originally from Brooklyn, from a family of six girls. We all were sexually abused by our drunken father. Mother died during the birth of my baby sister, Mable. Dad and I took care of all of us until he remarried. Dad was not a very godly man. Remember he molested me. After mom died, there were smutty women at the house all the time. Some of them were dirty and smelled, and others had long cigarette holders, and they always drank with Dad, when they went into the bedroom. When the women came out fully dressed hours later, I was the one who had to go in and check on him. Always he was there, lying on the bed snoring…naked. His empty billfold was open on the floor. I think that he felt as empty then, as I do now."

"You poor thing," the doctor says sympathetically, "but now our time is almost over."

(I bet he's thanking God for that.) "Susan, would you pray with me again as we end this session?"

Again I nod, and he continues, "Please, Lord, forgive us all, especially Susan and her father. Help them to understand the grace in Your forgiveness. Amen, Amen and Amen…Susan, make another appointment with the receptionist. "

Dr. Jones shakes my hand, as I leave, but he does not get up from his chair. I imagine that he does not want to display the erection that he undoubtedly has.

I make another appointment with the receptionist, as I slowly button the top button on my blouse. I walk out of the stifling office into the cool air, feeling good about what I had done.

During the taxi ride home, I think about what I had done and wondered what Christianity is really all about. But I feel calm because I know that I had done what I was supposed to do.

Chapter Two

For my second session with Dr. Jones, I again carefully pick out my clothes. Since the fall weather persists in chilling, I chose a satin blouse, a more revealing style of satin panties, a sweater and a long brown, fall skirt, which is cut much the same as last time with a long slit up the front. (Last season I saw a similar skirt without the slit, featured in the Neiman Marcus online catalog for almost four hundred dollars. The slit costs more.) I spend a long time combing my long, brown hair, and it falls perfectly and comfortably to my waist.

Before I enter the door, I check myself... everything. Perfect. When I enter the waiting room, the receptionist gives me a sly smile and motions me to sit down. So sit, I do...in my usual sexual way on the nearest hard, green, uncomfortable chair.

I notice something about Dr. Jones' receptionist this time that I missed before. Although she a little plump and wears a simple housedress, her brown eyes and dark hair shine. I begin to almost like her with her complicated combination of being innately sexy and working at not being sexy. She reminds me of a young woman that goes to church on Sunday morning, but then really has some juiced up sexy fun Sunday afternoon.

Sitting here is boring. I wait longer this time. From behind the door, leading to the offices, I hear a woman crying and a man yelling something. It sounds like, "Forget about the stupid affair and get on with your life."

The door opens, and it is the same couple from last time. When the man notices me, he stops yelling and gapes at me, but the woman just keeps sobbing.

"Don't you know that it a sin to have an affair?" she snorts through her weeping. She looks so dowdy and dismal and unkempt. No wonder he had the affair. But she keeps blubbering about their two children and asking him what is going to happen to them. He doesn't offer a response to her questioning; he just keeps gaping at me.

Finally the receptionist with an embarrassed half-smile and a shrug of her shoulders motions me through the open door to go find my own way back to Dr. Jones.

As I peek into his office, I see that this time, Dr. Jones is standing up, looking a bit disheveled.

"Was the last session a hard one?" I ask in a soothing, soft, quite motherly way.

"Even though I read from the Bible, I cannot convince him not to get a divorce. Divorce and affairs are sins, you know," he explains.

"Oh, is there anything I can do to help?" I inquire supportively.

"Thank you, Susan, but no. Please just give me a moment to compose myself."

"Sure," I whisper, as I reach out to him with my left hand. He touches my hand briefly, leaves the room. I hear him shut the door down the hall and hear water running. I imagine him in the bathroom where he is probably peeing, combing his hair, tucking his shirt into his slacks and throwing some cold water on his face.

When he comes back into his small office, Dr. Jones asks that we pray together again, I nod, and he begins.

"Dear Heavenly Father, please understand our human weaknesses and forgive our sins. And forgive the Petersons for the trouble that they are having, particularly Mr. Peterson who does not understand the sins involved in his affair, and, Father, help me be a better therapist now with Susan Mullins and be able to offer her what she really needs. Amen and Amen!"

He seems to feel better after the prayer, but he just broke a confidence about his previous clients.

Now he notices how I am sitting, nothing new just the same as before.

Because it is so warm in here, I ask, "Do you mind, Dr. Jones, if I take my sweater off?"

He nods, and I slowly and sexily struggle to slip off my sweater, making sure that he notices my every movement. He smiles, this time it is a warm, alluring smile, almost compassionate but very hungry.

How can I tell if a smile is hungry? He simply looks like he wants to come over and eat me up. It's not like a lover's smile but more like lust. Give me more of you, like he wishes that he was in my pants right now.

We talk rapidly during this session. About my sexual addiction as I again slowly and seductively unbutton the top button of my satin blouse. He talks about his wife, how they aren't happy together and how he decided on Christian counseling, as a way to prevent himself from getting too intimate with his clients.

It seems that Christian counseling has become a powerful protection for him, and as he talks I became more aware of the lonely pain that he feels. He has the same hunger that I do, but he has not resolved it, only covered it up with Biblical rhetoric, which only some of the time is meaningful to him.

"Can God love sexually, Dr. Jones?" I ask, knowing that most people, including therapists, do not like to think that God became true man through Jesus and that He certainly could have experienced love sexually.

He reminds me, "Now God is God, and God never has sex with anyone."

I remind him, "What about the recent book, Jesus' Room?"

He ignores me, as if he were thinking… deeply.

Suddenly his fire bell of a phone rings. I hear his receptionist scolding him across the room, "Dr. Jones, you've gone over your appointment time by ten minutes, and your next client is waiting."

His face flushes as he hangs up the phone without answering her. "We'd better pray," he stammers.

I nod.

"Dear God in Heaven, help us to solve Susan's problems and help all of us sinners to repent and experience the glories of Heaven. Amen. Amen."

As he escorts me down the hall from his office to the reception area, in quite a friendly way, I whisper, "Maybe we ought to have coffee sometime."

"No," he is emphatic, as he opens the door and then loudly shuts it once I've cleared the hallway.

During my taxi ride back to my loft, I tried to figure out what had just happened during that session. Dr. Jones had let his emotional hair down, had betrayed the Petersons' trust in him, had told me that he and his wife were not getting along, and it was obvious that I turned him on. I felt a little twinge in my gut and noticed that my panties were just a little bit wet. So I played with my crotch just a little to the embarrassment of the Pakistani taxi driver.

Finally inside my home I touch myself just once and have a massive climax. God, it felt so good, it almost hurt.

Chapter Three

The day of my next appointment is quite chilly and blustery, so I choose my outfit carefully. Satin panties, no bra, no pantyhose, a shiny white silk blouse, almost see-through but not quite, and another of my favorite, light wool skirts with a slit up the middle and the finest lining, certainly not a racy red lining but the quality I expect from Eileen Fisher or Ellen Tracy.

I sense this session will be different than the others, and I believe I'll be proven correct.

.

This time Dr. Jones is waiting for me in the waiting room. He is clean-shaven, wearing an attractive sports jacket and slacks, in brown tones that almost match and seemed to coordinate with the fall skirt that I was wearing. When he stands, turning to open the door to take me back to his office, the dowdy yet almost sexy receptionist smiles at me, quickly flashing a thumbs up, which

Dr. Jones does not notice. Knowing the standard meaning of the gesture, the message is like a beacon in the night telling me that I am sailing in the right direction

I follow him into his office and sit down like usual. After he takes his seat behind his little desk, I ever so slowly and sexily remove my sweater.

"Shall we pray?"

I nod, and he quickly continues, "Dear God in Heaven, please be mindful of your lost ones and help them to enter into the Kingdom of God, even though they have lost their way, have sinned in their thoughts, and not done Thy will. Amen. Amen."

That's a different twist of a prayer, more intense today, but it seems to include him this time, as well as me.

"What's happening?" he asks.

I tell him about how I hate living alone, that I masturbate when I feel lonely, because I live alone, and that I enjoyed drinking very fine wines and sometimes Appleton Special Gold- Jamaica Rum with Coke.

"Do you think you're an alcoholic?" he blurted out.

"I don't think so, but I could be. If I don't solve some of these problems, I could become one."

He nodded and smiled almost only to him, "I figured that you would be one who enjoyed fine wines. Are you a connoisseur? I don't know anything about wines."

No kidding! "Some wines sell for over $1,000.00 per bottle," I replied.

"Have you ever had that kind of wine?" he choked in amazement.

I nod and slowly unbutton the top button of my almost see-through blouse. I feel my nipples getting hard, and I am sure that he notices, too.

Dead silence for a moment, "Do you always dress like that?"

I just smile.

I feel the heat from his smile bouncing around his little office in an uncontrollable way, bouncing off the walls like an atom in an atom splitter.

"God you're beautiful!" he blurts out.

"Thank you," I respond, and then I revert back to our conversation about how I could become an alcoholic. But Dr. Jones is not listening. I do not know where his mind is, probably crawling around in my crotch.

"Times up," I say, looking at his clock on his desk, as I stand up. I slip on my sweater, button my blouse and rearranged my skirt, and I notice Dr. Jones' eyes following my every move and wonder if he is getting an erection.

He stands behind his small desk and stumbles as his foot catches on the desk leg as he walks around it, trying to divert attention from quarter-size wet spot on the front of his light brown pants. He guides me towards his office door.

With his hand on the door knob, I ask again, "Would you like to have coffee?"

This time he whispers softly with a very hungry and emphatic, "Yes."

"Chabellas next Thursday at eleven a.m.," confirming it with him then, taking his hand lovingly with my left hand, while turning the door knob with my right to exit his office.

Halfway down the hall, I hear his door slowly and quietly close. Next Thursday at eleven will be an interesting time!

My taxi rides back home are my special time for reflection and processing. I know Dr. Jones is interested, I know that he is unhappy, and I know that he is thinking about my satin panties and possibly what is under them. Thinking about this made my crotch wet and I notice that my satin panties were just a little wet, again.

Once inside my loft, with a little help from my dildo, I climax again magnificently.

Chapter Four

Thursday morning I get to Chabellas early so I can get the booth in the darkest corner of the bar. I know Dr. Jones will come. There's no question in my mind, so I am on purpose not wearing a bra or panties, but from the outside I look just like a Catholic girl going to church. Today I am wearing my pleasant, middle class, navy blue skirt from J.C. Penney's with a stiffly starched white cotton blouse, buttoned to the neck. Before I left the house I put two pairs of my satin panties in my purse before I left the house.

At precisely eleven, in walks Dr. Jones. I stand up and wave, so he can slide in the booth, and I can sit on the outside of the booth. He looks nice and seems glad to see me.

We make small talk for a few minutes, but then we have to order something. We decide on coffee; there are so many choices. I order the cold Mexican frappe with a touch of cinnamon; Dr. Jones obviously is having a very hard time deciding, so he asks for the same as mine. I know he has no idea what he will be served.

Our talk during coffee focuses mainly on the coffee and some of our therapy sessions. Then in a very professional way, Dr. Jones asks, "Susan, why did you want to have coffee?"

I gently, slowly open the two middle buttons of my blouse and ask him if he wants to touch my breasts.

Quietly but very emphatically he answers, "Yes." Discreetly and gently he slides his right hand into my blouse and slowly massages my nipples, which are already hard. As easily as his hand slipped into my blouse, Dr. Jones emotionally moved into another world, a private world of his own extracts. He smiles, and I assume he is probably imagining his own real world with me in it at the same time.

In a whisper, I ask him if he wants like to fondle my pussy.

He smiles and responds, "Yes," automatically putting his left hand between my thighs. Without him being aware, I have already pulled up my go-to-church skirt.

It feels good to me, and I let it happen for a while. Obviously, he has an erection so I ask him to open his pants. He carefully unzips and then I offer him a pair of my satin panties and ask if he would like to rub them on his penis. With a soft smile he hoarsely says, "Yes!" Slowly at first and then with a quiet groan or two he came and let his head fall back against the back of the high booth. He comes, he is spent, exhausted.

A few moments later, I ask, "Would you like to do that again sometime?"

He smiles, as he sighs, "Yes!"

I whisper with my lips barely touching his ear, as I give him the other pair of satin panties that I had put in my purse, "I will be in touch with you, but during our next meeting you must wear these satin panties!"

Quietly he smiles, "Yes."

Before I stand up, I make sure my blouse is buttoned and my skirt straight and proper. Then I get up, make my way through the darkened bar to the waitress, give her a large tip and ask her, "Please do not bother him for a little while." She agrees, and I leave Chabellas.

I hail a taxi. What fun, as I sat on the well warn black leather back seat. I really got the "hots," and I think that I came. Anyway there was a wet spot on the back seat and the taxi driver bitched at me for peeing on the seat. Little did he know what had really happened.

Chapter Five

By now, I assume you know I'm a woman of independent means. That is true, but I am not pretentious. I live in a two level loft in Old Towne in Philadelphia. (I also keep a condo in Chicago near the Lake front.) My loft is furnished in the sparse Scandinavian style, following all the rules of Fung Shui. It suits me quite well and I find it very cozy and balanced. My closets are filled with expensive clothes that I use for various occasions.

I don't go out a lot, but I do sometimes bring something in to eat like chicken or fish. I do not work for anyone, although I sometimes volunteer for United Way and a few other causes. Some of my money was left to me by my parents, but most of my money, about $200,000.00 per month comes from my cottage industry—apparel design...not just any clothes. I sell exclusively on my member only Internet site. I have a broker in New York who does all the marketing work for me, and I pay him well. Believe me, I pay him well, but he works hard.

I also love animals and have a short-haired cat who thinks that I am her friend. But sex is my life. I am constantly thinking and reading about it. Sometimes I masturbate, and sometimes I need a man like Dr. Jones.

I also like flowers, all kinds of flowers and some kinds of vegetables. On the roof of the loft, I have a greenhouse and garden section. This is a green building, which is handy for those of us who like to get our hands really dirty.

During the short summer, I grow leeks, which I order from Jung Flowers. They work so much better than onions or scallions for soups and salads. I also grow some daises and have an uncontrollable vine of Chinese Wisteria. My other flower patches, include beautiful day lilies, some early tulips and a miniature Burning Bush, which is a very beautiful red in the late fall. It was supposed to be miniature, but it has grown taller than me and sometimes overshadows the rest of my little garden.

I have a gardener that I call "Jim." Jim and I have had an affair a couple of times. I like to sit and watch him work, while wearing no panties and allowing my skirt to open. It drives him wild. A little red wine and my crotch is enough recompense for him.

Every spring I have a little party, La Dolce Vita style. It's to celebrate the melting of the snow and the welcoming openness of spring. Spring costumes, complete with masks or other headgear are imperative, so my guests can only guess who they are having sex with. I make wines of all varieties, from less expensive local wineries to expensive imports, but I prohibit hard liquor. This is a sex party and not a drunken brawl. Everybody comes at exactly the same time. Couples mix, so no one knows exactly what is happening with whom until exactly two in the morning. That's when everyone takes off their masks and goes home with their spouse or someone else's spouse or someone who came without a formal invitation.

That happens often and one year a well-known local politician showed up uninvited, and everyone was surprised, especially Martha, when the clock chimed two. I, however, never participate sexually in these parties. I just observe.

This kind of party is much better that watching X-rated movies, like my old favorite, Beyond the Green Door. This is because my guests get to act it out mysteriously themselves and not just sit around, masturbating with someone we know, while watching a dull, x-rated, movie with no plot. Many special friendships have been made at these parties. People can switch partners, but it is hard to hide the identifying tattoos that they may have on their genitals. One of my regular attendees has a large snake tattoo on his penis. Everyone laughs when it springs to life and spits out its venom.

As you can imagine the second story of my loft is furnished with everything—comfortable chairs, couches, erotic lighting, pillows and some tastefully-done, sexually stimulating, seductive pictures. But there's nothing obscene. Most of the time I sit around the loft by myself, but sometimes I throw a party. I don't like to talk on the telephone because it is so sterile. Have you ever had real sex with someone over the telephone? Disgusting, isn't it.

But you ought to see my bathroom. It's quite large and very sexy with a whirl pool tub, the manufacturer calls it Cleopatra, and it's in my favorite bathroom color, biscuit. I designed the exotic lighting, and I ordered specially designed mirrors all around the room, including on the bottom of the bath tub, and flameless candles with some special erotic scents that turn on or off just by waving your hand. You cannot get away from sex in my bathroom because the mirrors reflect into infinity. It's like every inch of you is exposed to the whole world all of the time.

The room also includes a toilet, bidet, a large sink and make up area all filled with the same kinds of mirrors. When I stand up to go pee it's like I am peeing on the whole world. Our world really needs to be peed on right now, and that is the only political statement that I will make. I promise.

I get turned on just entering my bath sanctuary, and sometimes I come naturally just being there. It is my favorite place, especially after one of my parties. They use up so much of my energy, but they are so-o-o fun to put on.

Chapter Six

It's late spring and I am horny again.

Back to searching the *Yellow Pages*. There the name Raymond Larson, M.D., PhD, Freudian Analyst, jumps out at me. Now he sounds really important! I call, and I'm told he has had an unusual last minute cancellation, because his patient was called out of the country for a few months. He can see me tomorrow without the usual six week wait.

So I very carefully pick a bra and a blouse that when the top button is unbuttoned reveals the most that is politely possible and a crepe, ruffled skirt that has a hem right at the knees. I wear my usual satin panties with no stockings.

As I opened his heavy oaken door to his office for my Tuesday morning appointment at 10:00, I am aware of a massive opulent waiting room with very new and expensive pictures and thick carpeting and the smell of leather. The receptionist sits up board straight and has small horned-rimmed glasses that sit on the edge of her nose. She wears a proper grey suit, with a proper light blue blouse buttoned to her neck. She goes about her "work," and I watch her a few minutes, as I wait. What is under that stiff manikin? I bet ya, I know.

As I enter his large lavishly furnished office, which he can easily afford at his $500.00 hourly fee, a the large chandelier, obviously beautifully made of hand blown glass from the famous island of Murano, hangs from the high plaster and wood ceiling. The very beautiful silk and wool pile, hand-knotted rug, which appears to be Isfahan from Iran, covers a corner of the room, surrounded by three over-stuffed, leather chairs and a luxurious upholstered, large, welcoming couch. The quality of the workmanship is reflected in its lack of wear. Although it has been used many times over the years, there is no sign of wear.

Dr. Larson invites me to take my shoes off and to lie down on the couch and put my head on a pillow which he fluffs up. Dr. Larson, an older man in his late sixties has a provocative, large mustache which does not move when he talks.

I follow his instructions seductively, kicking my shoes slightly as I take them off and making sure that my skirt makes a crumpling noise when I lie down. As I put my head down, I make sure that my long hair falls across the pillow seductively.

I ask, "What's next?"

Dr. Larson sits at the head of the couch out of my line of sight and tells me to "Close your eyes and tell me whatever is on your mind."

So I start, "I have a sexual problem. I want help because sex is running my life."

"Oh," comes from behind me.

I proceed, "I constantly think about sex. I was abused as a little girl by my older brother and my father. When I was eleven, both my brother and my father, on many separate occasions had ripped my panties off and both always threatened me not to tell my mother, who was especially stern, because she would beat the piss out of me."

I pause and then continue, "In Junior High some of the boys would gather under the bleachers, after the games or assemblies, trying see the girls' underpants. I could hear them giggling, so I decided not to wear underpants anymore except when I had my periods. Then I would stand there straddling the gape in the bleachers so the boys could get a real good look at what they wanted to see.

As I talk I gently unbutton the top button of my blouse and almost immediately I feel and smell the hot, smoky breath of Dr. Larson on my round breasts, but I keep my eyes closed. Dr. Larson has been typing away on his Toshiba laptop. I noticed it leaning against the chair at the head of the couch, when I first came in. I assume he holds it on his lap, and he's been typing non-stop, since I started talking. His typing really bothers me because I want to see what is in his notes on the computer.

I continue telling him about my lesbian experiences and how I for a time thought that I was a lesbian…

But he clears his throat interrupting me in mid-sentence and tapping me on my head. At first I think he has a pencil, but then ever so gently I feel his fingers touching my hair, as he says, "Your fifty minutes are up. The receptionist will make another appointment for tomorrow."

After I sit up, I hand him five crisp $100 bills from the pocket of my skirt and ask, "Tomorrow?"

"Yes, analysis is an intense process, and we have to do it everyday until you are healthy."

Hum, everyday could be fun but expensive.

Chapter Seven

I choose my clothes wisely for this afternoon's appointment... an uplift satin bra, satin panties, a spring like skirt cut deeply up the middle, a silk frilly blouse- one of my favorites—no stockings, and some plain deep brown, buttery leather flats.

When I finally get to Dr. Larson's waiting room I am still amazed at the quality of the furnishings and the paintings. I have some originals in my home but not of the quality of Dr. Larson's. The pipsqueak receptionist is still here, wearing what appears to be the same tailored suit and maintaining the same stiff posture. I look to see if she is breathing. Has she moved a muscle since yesterday?

She finally buzzes me into Dr. Larson's office. He is in the same position in the chair at the head of the couch, in the same rumpled suit and shirt. He appears to have aged since yesterday, and this visit so far seems like a macabre dream. It's like

I've entered a mysterious wax museum. Is he a wax figure, as well, or is he real?

"Please take off your shoes," he says without his moustache moving, "Lie down on the couch." He has a pillow prepared. It is fresh smelling, like the pillows found in finest hotels. As I lay down, my hair falls perfectly over the pillow, and the left half of my skirt falls off the couch, almost revealing my satin panties, if someone were to enter Dr. Larson's office now and see us, they would think that we were about to have an affair.

"Continue," he says.

"I have been thinking of penises a lot lately. I have seen hundreds of them, you know, big, little, commanding and disappointing. All were soft and pink. I like to take the balls in my hand and gently massage them, like the famous Chinese steel relaxation balls, but my massage of them is always gentle, tender and kind."

"When the penis begins to slowly elongate, it turns me on, but all I want to do is give pleasure to men," I continue as I open the top button of my blouse. "I can't help but think of your penis, how nice and gentle but firm it must be, because you are always helping people. It must be uncomfortable for your penis as you sit in the same chair with your same computer warming your lap, day after day, listening to sad stories like mine."

I can hear Dr. Larson's breathing cycles increase, and sometimes I sense his hot, smoky breath on my breasts. I think he touched my hair once, but I am not sure.

After a long pause, I tell him, "Sometimes I like to put my hair up, dress like a man and go into men's washrooms and watch them pee and primp. Don't you ever think that a man doesn't primp. Sometimes they have a hard time getting their penises back into their pants. Some even get them caught in their zippers. Ouch! They must be ever so careful when they zip up their pants.

Some of the men I've observed wash their hands very deliberately and comb their hair. But some men just leave the washroom without washing their hands. It's as if these mean-spirited men want to get the germs from their penises on the first woman they meet. It's like they want to violate her in a way that she will have no way of understanding or even being aware of. That disgusts me, because I am always clean and fresh and use my bidet at least twice a day."

"I always change my panties at least twice a day for sanitary reasons, too, and sometimes one of my male companions will ask to have the satin panty that I just took off."

I'm sure he touched my hair this time, and his breathing is more rapid and raspy. He almost gurgles in desperation.

"Did I tell you about my web site?"

"Time's up," Dr. Larson interrupts.

But I don't want to leave right now because he sounded like he was going to have a heart attack or stroke. So I slowly and seductively get off his expensive couch, adjust my skirt and button my blouse and turn to look at him. Quickly Dr. Larson quiets down, either to get rid of me or to go masturbate in his bathroom. I leave the five crisp $100 bills on the pillow.

He says nothing other than, "See you tomorrow," as I put on my shoes, walked across the room, opened the door and left.

During the cab ride home, I felt kind of uneasy but couldn't quite identify what I was feeling. Was I upset? No. Was I depressed? No. I guess that I was angry. Angry at what this old lecher, Dr. Larson, is doing. Years and years on his couch at $500.00 per hour would be very expensive and where would it get me as far as my sexual problem goes. Do I really have a million dollar problem?

Chapter Eight

The next day I bathed with delicately scented oils before my appointment with Dr. Larson. After I dried off, I put on my most revealing satin, thong panties. As I was leaving his office yesterday, I saw a small mirror placed inconspicuously on the table at the foot of the couch, where he thought I wouldn't notice it, but where he could see up my skirt. I put on my extreme push-up bra, but I could not decide on my skirt. I didn't want to be too obvious. So I put on a soft, light blue skirt cut as usual and a clinging light weight, v-necked, button-up spring sweater.

After I dried my hair, had a cup of coffee, and checked myself one more time in the mirror, I stuck a pair of clean satin panties in my purse.

As I enter the reception area, it is very bright and sunny from the two skylights in the ceiling. I guess that I had come before on dark days because I hadn't noticed the two skylights. Nothing else had changed, including the receptionist. I'm guessing that she is most definitely a wax figure, operated by some remote control or electrical device. Again, she buzzes me into Dr. Larson's office.

"Please take off your shoes. Now lie down on the couch and close your eyes."

I did so seductively making sure that part of my skirt again fell on the floor and that my hair was just right. I felt my tanned long legs glistening in the dimmed light as if they were beacons to my crotch.

"Begin."

"Yesterday I was going to tell you about my web site. It's very sexually titillating but discrete, as well."

I mention my hair and how much it means to me. "I can't tell you how many men I've seduced by dangling my long hair on their genitals. I especially liked to squirt melted chocolate around my belly button and have a nude man lick if off, after I have tied his hands behind his back or to the bed frame."

I hold nothing back from Dr. Larson. But as I talk, I am aware that I like sex in as many ways as it is possible to have sex.

While I'm talking, I listen to the click, click of his computer, supposedly documenting all that I am saying. Hell, it would be much easier to use a tape recorder; then Dr. Larson could sleep during our sessions.

Now I'm aware of a different rhythm of his key board. Usually it was an uneven rhythm, because what I was saying, but now the rhythm of his key board clicking became even and predictable.

At-a, tatata, tatat. At, tatata, Tatata.

The typing stopped completely right in the middle of one of my sentences. "Don't you like what I was saying," I asked.

No response.

Again, I asked, "You stopped typing. Don't you like what I was saying?"

No response.

Maybe he's dead from lack of circulation, sitting in that chair, clutching that hot little laptop all these years. Could I have bored him to death?

I slowly and seductively get up. Not sure what I'll see, I turn to find Dr. Larson looking like he was in a daze, something between a drug high and a trance. I lift the computer off his lap and read "I want her. I want her, I want her."

I guess that I did make an impression after all. Looking down I notice that the zipper on his pants was open, so I touch the open crotch and out popped the smallest, prune-like penis that I have ever seen… all shriveled up, and I couldn't see his balls at all.

I opened my clutch bag and placed the extra pair of panties on his penis and said, "Please wear these panties during our session next time." He just looked at me, half-smiling, but saying nothing. After I picked up my shoes, I walked to the door, then slipped on my shoes and left, locking the door from the inside.

During the taxi ride home I decided that I was up to my old tricks again and smiled to myself, I wonder what will happen in our next session. Just about anything could and probably will.

Chapter Nine

"Spring is in the air, and I feel good." Now I'm talking to myself. For this session, I'm wearing a spring outfit. A very low cut top, another push-up bra from Victoria's Secret, a springy light green skirt with no slit and a slight green ruffle, my white satin panties and my white ballet flats with a dainty buckle. My long brown hair compliments my light green skirt. "I look fine," talking to myself again.

Standing by the door to Dr. Larson's office, I wonder what is going to happen next. When I open the door, and see the same waiting room with the expensive pictures and the same straight-laced receptionist, not smiling and not scowling, just seemingly waxen, frozen in time.

When she buzzes me into his office, I detect a slight smile on her lips, but it is not a real smile. It's more like, aha! I gotcha, I see right through you. As I stand at his office door, with the door wide open I see the same little man with the same clothes, sitting in the same place. So I stand with my feet firm, wide apart, with my hands on my hips, and ask loud enough for the receptionist to hear, "Do you have my panties on?"

"No," he whispers, shaking his head.

"Go put them on," I say with the door still open.

"Yes," he responds.

He leaves for some place, as I close the door to the hallway. Then I take my place at the head of the couch in his chair. He comes back a few minutes later, and I ask again, "Do you have my panties on?"

"Yes," he nods.

And then I tell him, "Take your place on the couch."

He lies down obediently and becomes the patient, and I become his master. He has taken his jacket off and his wrinkled dirty white shirt and wrinkled pants imply that he has not moved from his chair for years. "Are you ready?" I ask.

"Yes."

"What we are going to do will be lots of fun, but you must follow my instructions very clearly! Imagine that you are on the thirty- third floor of a building."

"But I am afraid of heights."

"Shut up and do what I say!"

"Yes," he mummers.

"You are entering a glassed-in elevator on the thirty-third floor of your favorite hotel, the door of the elevator closes and you look around for the down button. You push the lobby button and then sit on the floor of the elevator. This is a special elevator because it moves ever so slowly, very smoothly but slowly. As you sit on the floor of the elevator you close your eyes and, believe it or not, begin to immediately relax, because you know I am taking care of you.

"Thirty-second floor, the relaxation falls over your entire body, from the top of your head to bottom of your feet.

"Thirty-first floor, more and more relaxed. You are beginning to enjoy feeling relaxed. It is a relaxation that you have never felt before.

"Thirtieth floor, your ears and nose are particularly relaxed.

"Twenty- ninth floor.

"Twenty-eighth floor. So comfortable. Breathing in relaxation, breathing out tension, breathing in relaxation, breathing out tension.

"Twenty- seventh floor. Every part of your body is relaxing, so quiet, so relaxed.

"Twenty- sixth floor.

"Twenty-fifth floor. While your whole body is relaxed, you are beginning to feel a slight tingling in your penis, that penis which is covered with my panties, my satin panties. Do you feel it? Yes, of course, you do.

"Twenty-fourth floor.

"Twenty- third floor. You relax even more, and your whole body can not move, except your penis with its little twitching.

"Twenty-second floor.

"Twenty-first floor. You are beginning to see my face, my beautiful long brown hair, my breasts.

"Twentieth floor. ...my breasts, which are just the right size, not too big, not too small, just the right size. Just for you.

"Nineteenth floor. You remember looking at my panties in your mirror, my satin panties and wondering what is underneath them

"Eighteenth floor. There is something strange brewing inside of you. Essentially it begins in your penis but, even though you cannot move, the excitement you feel is beginning to tingle in your ears and on the top of your nose.

"Seventeenth floor. You can actually see me. I am taking off my clothes for your pleasure. For your pleasure.

"Sixteenth floor. My blouse comes off slowly, button by button. Then slipping to the floor.

"Fifteenth floor. You can't stand it. You are begging to see the tips of my breasts, my sweet, succulent breasts, you want to touch them. You want to kiss them, but you can't move. You see me only in your mind as your penis begins to tingle more and more, and it is all beginning to drive you sexually mad.

"Fourteenth floor. Slowly my skirt slips down, falling over my knees, landing on the floor.

"Thirteenth floor. I kick my skirt away, and all I have on is my panties, panties just like yours.

"Twelfth floor. I'm touching my crotch, Dr. Larson.

"Eleventh floor. You want to touch your crotch, but you can't yet. Be a good boy, Dr. Larson, just let you penis grow and tingle a little at a time, as it begins to push at the satin of my panties.

"Tenth floor. You fall deeper and deeper relaxed and now you are beginning to feel a sexual urgency in your penis, a sexual urgency that you have not felt since you wore your mother's panties, and she helped masturbate you. But I am not your mother; I am a beautiful, attractive woman who is raping you.

"Ninth floor. God, you want to be raped.

"Eighth floor. Your penis is beginning to push hard against your satin panties.

"Seventh floor. Good God, you feel excited!

"Sixth floor. We are nearing the end of our journey, Dr. Larson, and you know it. You look forward to it. It will be like a wonderful explosion. Dr. Larson.

"Fifth floor. Oh, God.

"Fourth floor. This is the beginning of our sexual end, Dr. Larson. You are beginning to feel your hands and arms tingling, Dr. Larson, and they are beginning to move.

"Third floor. You know what is going to happen next, don't you, Dr. Larson. Yes…

"Second floor. Your penis is bigger now than it ever has been, Dr. Larson, it's throbbing with pain, sexual pain, a pain that you haven't felt in years. Dr. Larson, you have held it in for so many years. Dr. Larson, during these many years, you have become a voyeur, wishing, watching, thinking, hallucinating. Dr. Larson, you want me and your receptionist. Dr. Larson, it hurts so badly but in just a moment the whole world will explode.

"Ground floor. Dr Larson, I want you to unzip your pants, reach inside your pants and pullout that throbbing penis and rub it and rub it until it explodes all over, like a fountain. Dr. Larson, rub it. Rub it. Hard, Dr. Larson.

"There you go, Dr Larson, semen all over the place, on you, on the walls of the elevator and all over those women who have entered the elevator with their satin panties and their long brown hair. They are really something. Dr. Larson, they are licking your semen and admiring your satin panties.

"Dr Larson, it's time to begin thinking about waking you now. I am going to count back to floor thirty- three and by the time we get to thirty- three, you will be wide awake and very aware of all that has happened.

"Beginning now…

"1,2,3,4,5,6…7,8,9,10,11,12…13,14,15,16,1 7,18,19,20…21,22,23,24…getting awake 25, 26, more slowly now, 27. 28. 29….30, 31, 32. 33. Wide awake."

Slowly Dr. Larson began to sit up.

"Oh Dr. Larson, you wet your satin panties."

There is a long pause while things calm down. "There is semen all over you, Dr. Larson, and all over your very expensive couch." Dr Larson looks like a banana split covered in whipped cream.

"I came," he said in disbelief, happy but embarrassed at the same time. He seems to see me both as his mother and a Playboy model at the same time. He reaches out to hold me, but I refuse, backing away. Besides he is a mess!

Soon Dr. Larson smiles kind of a silly-ass, smile and disappears through the door on the other side of his office, which I assume is his private bathroom. I take out another pair of my satin panties and put them on his chair. Without knocking I open his private door, tell him to wear the new satin panties the next time I see him, shut the door and leave.

Back in the reception area, the receptionist broadly smiles and says, "Thank you." I wonder what she means. She is not a wax figurine after all.

During the taxi ride home I feel angry at myself. I have done it again, but I still have not solved my own problem. My problem has to do with sex. Even as a clothes designer, my company constantly markets only one thing—sex. But I often wonder if my sexual designs are really for men or for the women that wear them.

As you know, a bunch of young, female, "entertainers" have been in trouble lately for drinking, drugs, nudity and raucous behavior. Maybe this whole scene including me is getting out of hand.

Chapter Ten

When I return to my loft in Old Towne, Escabelle, my dear, life-long friend, waits for me. I see her Audi A6 Advant parked down the block as I arrive. We had set this time to plan my late summer party. I want the theme to be Early Halloween: a costume ball.

Escabelle already has an X-Rated Fusion half gone, when I walk in. There is no telling how many she has consumed before I arrived, not to say that she has a problem with liquor or anything. We chat but the time for real party planning has already past...except we decide there will be some kind prize for the winning costume.

Escabelle and I always have fun together, giggling and romping around together. She, like me, is tall, but while I look strong, probably because I work out almost daily, she is tall and skinny. To me Escabelle looks weak and a bit undernourished, but she doesn't like it when I tell her that.

How can we really plan anything lying around naked on the bed together drinking? There's no sex involved; we both just need to be close. But no candy store Fusions for me. I like my Martinis. I know it won't be long before we are asleep…as usual.

`The next morning we wake up long after the day is bright and shiny, a bit groggy but feeling refreshed, if that kind of incongruous feeling is possible. We quickly dress, kiss and are off, going our separate ways.

Chapter Eleven

The next to the last Saturday in August, the party is all set, thanks to my staff who knows how to work well with Escabelle's employees. Frankly I've been far too busy with the company designing, preparing for next spring shows, and reviewing the Chicago marketing campaigns to think of party planning. Escabelle, who runs a very successful boutique around the corner from my loft is simply too lazy to do but finds it easier to delegate. I think she is far better off than I am, but I can't prove it. She has a sexual problem, too, but that's another story.

The guests arrived and what a variety of costumes. Zorro with Queen Elizabeth (what a combination!) and Peter the Pig accompanies Elizabeth Taylor. But the winning costume was the elephant with a big head and an oversized penis for a trunk, erect, of course. Inserted in the body of the elephant, between the front legs and the back legs there is a shadow-box like insertion, with a miniature sculpture, depicting a man with a woman behind him sucking on his balls, coupled with a man behind her. It was so funny and strange that I am still laughing and dreaming about it. God, what a party! Of course, the albino boa constrictor was there, as always brought by his owner.

Class, whatever that means, is very important to me. But you might ask, what is class? Is it a bunch of people of privilege having sexual fun together? For some that might be class, because of their bank accounts they feel that they have not only the license but also the means to act on their desires. But to me, class really means someone who is motivated not only to have fun but also to be successful. Very few of my guests have nine-to-five jobs. Some do infomercials on television, while others do nothing that resemble commerce of any kind. The key is an attitude, a profession or the knowledge that you exhibit style in all that you do.

Real class is knowing how to use your panties, your body and your mind. I never have sex with a man or woman, for that matter, at any of these parties. I only play around with Escabelle and that really isn't sexual. People seem to think that Escabelle and I are lesbians, but we've not. So, I do have a genuine sexual problem.

Chapter Twelve

In late September and early October the sexual need pattern in me starts to manifest itself again. I feel the need for therapy again, after all sex for me is getting out of hand. I have tried so many social workers, psychologists, marriage and family therapists and psychiatrists that I don't know where to turn to get the help that I really need, which is something new and different for me.

I decide on an individual at one of the training universities in the Chicago area. It needs to be a place that trains all kinds of disciplines and also has a Medical School. Finally I find just what I want, a PhD-seeking psychologist in his fourth year of training. Psychologists like social workers and all the others have what is called, Field Work, where they actually get hands-on training seeing people, like me. But they really don't see people, they see problems. His name is John Nicole.

John, as I mentioned, is a fourth year student in a Ph.D. Psychology program. Since he is an intern, he seeks office space anywhere that he can find it. When I called for an appointment, he told me his office was in a physician's examining room at one of the hospitals, not far from the Loop.

After searching high and low and getting lost at least four times, I finally find his temporary office, Room 616B. It is on the sixth floor of a wing of that vast hospital that is not attached to the main lobby of the hospital.

As I stand in front of 616B, amidst the hustle and bustle of this teaching hospital, I am wearing a sheer white blouse, a white bra a long skirt with the usual slit and black satin panties. I knock, and John opens the door, commenting, "You're a little late for our session."

"You betcha I'm a little late. You're a hard man to find."

He smiled and ushered me into his "office" which consists of an examining table complete with stirrups, two hard chairs and a bunch of medical stuff like a blood pressure cuff, a colorful chart of the stages of birth and a Surgeon General's warning against smoking while pregnant, as well as the anatomical posters of breasts and vaginas. How hard up must John Nicole be to select the distracting OBGYN examining room for his temporary office.

John is a neat looking guy. But he seems very young, probably around twenty-six. God, he's young! He is wearing white slacks, white bucks, and a light brown shirt, dark brown tie and white lab jacket.

"Have a seat," he says, offering me one of the two hard chairs and sitting on the other one, which he had placed, in such a way that he could use the examining table as a desk of sorts. There was no simple way at all to be seductive on these hard, institutional, plastic chairs, but trust me, I will find a way.

After getting my name and address and some other demographics, which he called "social information," he asks, "What is your problem?"

I tell him about my sexual problems, how I love to watch sex, and how my father and brother had sexually abused me as a child. I also mention my hedonistic parties and describe the elephant with the penis for a trunk with the fucking sculpture inside. I share the humor I felt at the costume, and he sort of laughed, but not really. Was he trying to be polite?

As I talk, the future Dr. Nicole nods appropriately but does not say too much. He doesn't ask many questions, but near the end of the session, he asks, "What kind of help do you think that you need?"

"I don't really know," I say simply.

"Why don't I give you some tests next time for me to compare with others with the same kinds of problems that you have?" John asks.

I nod in agreement.

He pulls out his brand new Day-Timer, and we schedule another appointment. I can't help but notice how open his calendar appears. When he stands up, he hunches over. It was then that I noticed a small wet spot of the front of his white pants.

As I leave John's office, I realize I feel really hungry, so I'm off to find the hospital cafeteria. On my way down to the first floor on the elevator-and I hate taking elevators because I find them claustrophobic-I realize that I am on the maintenance elevator, ending up in the basement. After much difficulty finding the stairs up to the first floor, I ascend the stairwell up to the first floor, but the door is locked.

"Damn it!" I pound and pound on the metal door, feeling frantically trapped until a little old, ugly, toothless janitress with a mop in her hand, begrudgingly opens the door, shaking her head and mumbling, freeing me from my temporary prison.

I finally find the cafeteria and get a pop, wishing I carried a flask of vodka in my purse. I could use a drink….even coke and vodka. I select a rejected, wilted green salad, unfit for a wild rabbit to ingest, topped with hard boiled eggs. The cashier, with missing teeth like the janitress, tells me I get my choice of one dressing in a bag with the salad. The benefit package for this hospital must not include dental insurance. Why is it that hospitals have some of the worst benefits? You'd think that they would provide the best healthcare for their employees. Strange!

I leave the hospital and find a cab waiting near the entrance. I feel terrible about my pitiful lunch and what I had "unintentionally" done to the poor, young, student psychologist. He was kind of nice, too. Am I actually feeling guilt, or am I actually having perverted fun at his expense?

At my Chicago condo, I fix myself a double dry martini. "Shaken not stirred," pops in my mind and down it goes.

Chapter Thirteen

For my next appointment with John I dressed as un-sexy as I could. A simple broadcloth, cotton blouse, an up-lifting bra, my favorite Ann Taylor flowered skirt and black satin panties. I arrive on time, finding him with less trouble this time, and John is waiting for me. He's wearing blue slacks, an outdoorsman, strange tweed shirt, a Mickey Mouse tie and a white doctor's lab coat that didn't fit. He looks kind of funny, a bit like the little television Dr. Doogie Houser, who has to roll up the sleeves of his jacket because they are too long.

John has some tests laid out on the examining table. I see a test sheet with some open ended questions, a Sexual Check List, and a picture test that he called the Thematic Appreciation Test. I, like a good girl, take his tests. The open-ended question test is first, and when I look up I see him looking at my hair, which I tried to fix as sexily as possible, long and silky. Once in a while his hand accidentally brushes against my hair or his knee accidentally touches my knee. He's sitting on my side of the examining table for the testing.

As I take the open-ended question test, I catch him looking at my hair, with a kidlike, longing look, like something is missing in his life. I wonder what it is that he could be missing. I think that John was probably not nurtured by his parents, so I ask right in the middle of my test, "Are you married, John?"

"No," he answered, like a steer being lead to the slaughter.

After I finish all tests, he asks, "Would you like to go down for coffee, while I score these, and come back in an hour?"

"No, I'll just wait here, thank you."

After about 45 minutes he's done, and without consulting his supervisor, he tells me, "Susan, you have an addiction to sex."

"How can I be addicted to sex, John? Sex is fun," I asked.

We talk for a while, and then he looks at the clock and realizes that we have gone way over time. "I'm really sorry, Susan, but you have to leave now," he apologizes rather pitifully.

As I get up I notice a bigger wet spot on the front of his pants. Has he actually come in his pants, while we were talking? He seems like such a nice boy.

No cafeteria this time. I take a direct ride home in the cab, with a funny feeling in my belly about John. I fix a double dry martini and a soak in a hot tub. And what a soak it was because I really needed to calm down. Or maybe it was the second double dry martini; I don't really remember, but I'm calmer now.

I think about John on and off all week. I sort of like him. Am I old enough to be his mother? But he is kind of cute, and he's not married and often during the week I wonder why he could possibly want to be a psychologist, to play in the sewer sludge of other people and their stinky problems.

I also met Escabelle a couple of times during the week, she likes to fly in when I come to Chicago, but she always stays near "Water Tower Place". We like to go out to eat and have a couple of drinks together. Our favorite spot is Dick's Bar and Grill. Contrary to its name, it really is a fancy restaurant that serves such delicacies as escargot, bouillabaisse, and snippy little finger sandwiches that taste like heaven. They also have the best dry martinis in town. Escabelle and I know most of the regulars there, but every once in a while a new customer will amble in wondering what the place is like. When that happens, we try to make the newbie's comfortable and maybe even sit and flirt with them.

I told Escabelle that I could not get John, with his wet pants off my mind. She laughed out loud and told me that I was getting old and really horny. Hell, I have been horny all my life, but to think sexually about John who is young enough to be my son is crazy. I do not have a son, I have never been married, but I have wanted to a couple of times. It just never worked out. I guess because I am so consumed with my design business and sex. By the way, I am going to have to fly to France one of these days to make sure Max is doing what he is supposed to be doing. I love Max, too, but we are making more money internationally than we are supposed to be making, and I wonder what he is up to.

I do have a cat, a wonderful tabby cat which is the friendliest animal in the world. She travels with me and meets me at the door when I come home, sits on my lap and sleeps in my bed with me. She is my friend, and I imagine that I am her friend. She is like the cat in the commercial for cat food, you know tap the crystal dish with the silver spoon, and she comes running...I feed her the best of everything that I can find, but she hates escargot.

Chapter Fourteen

Getting ready for my next appointment with John I intentionally leave off my bra and panties, put on a sheer, white low-cut, button down blouse and a white, see- through skirt which, if I am in just the right light, reveals everything.

I knock and very quickly John opens the door to his "office." I stand in the light so everything was revealed. I hear him gasp. Then with both feet planted on the ground I said, "Do you want to fuck?"

After a couple more gasps, he fainted in a crumpled heap right on the spot. Now I'm worried. Could he have had a heart attack?

I quickly look out the door, see a "white coat" a few feet away and yell, "Help me!" I guess she is a doctor, but she checks out the crumpled heap on the floor and reassures me that Dr. Nicole had only fainted and had not had a heart attack at all.

Thank God! I would never want to hurt John.

Within moments, thanks to the "white coat" administering some smelling salts, John begins to come around. John's face took the brunt of the fall, and now he looks like he's been run over by a million Arabian Nights.

The "white coat" with a very strong foreign accent had called out the door, "Orderly," the only word I could understand her to say. And now John's awake, lying on the examining table a folded towel under his neck and an ice pack on his forehead. The" white coat" mumbles something in a commanding voice, and she and the "orderly" leave the room shutting the door.

"What happened?"—the first words from John.

"You fainted," I respond, using my very gentle, reassuring, quiet motherly tone. "John, would you like to masturbate with one of my panties?"

"Oh, yes," he gulped, closing his eyes.

"Unzip you pants," I whisper.

"Yes," as he slowly took the zipper and unzipped his pants and out popped the largest swollen penis that I have ever seen.

"Here," as I give him one of my satin panties from my purse, and then turn to lock the door, "rub your penis with this."

He rubs slowly at first and then faster as he writhes on the examining table and in a few moments, I really have no idea how long, he comes and comes and comes, as if he has just been uncorked after years and years of being bottled up.

Gently I touch his forehead and ask, "Are you ok, John?"

"Yes," he responds with a heavy, rough tone to his voice, "Very OK."

Next to his head on the examining table, I place the other pair of my satin panties; I always carry a couple of spares. "Wear them the next time we meet," I whispered as I kiss his forehead gently and leave quietly.

So John could sleep the deep sleep of release, I lock the door from the inside as I leave and remove the "Examining Room Occupied" sign from the door knob across the hall, placing it on the door knob to John's temporary office.

Gawd, I felt good on the taxi ride home. For some reason I like John, he is so innocent, so out of control. A psychologist who is so unlike any psychologist I'd ever known. John is just a little boy. I know at least that I can turn him on; I wonder if he could turn me on.

Chapter Fifteen

After talking with Escabelle, once I returned from my work in Chicago, we decide to have a special party this year for our special international networking group, as we refer to it, poking fun at the local lead generating groups with chapters around the country. It would be a special party where no one would dress up. No gala, no bizarre costumes. Instead, everyone would dress down. Numbers would be randomly drawn and soft clean blue pillows would be provided for those randomly matched couples, who wanted to sit on the floor, play with or fuck with each other.

"What fun!" Escabelle giggles, but I know who she secretly plans to pair up with, and I know, like always she will "fix" the drawing in her favor. She is used to getting what she wants from whom she wants it. Just a bit spoiled—that girl!

I set the date and then send special invitations to my three special guests, John, Dr. Larson and

Mr. Peterson. They promptly and happily RSVP, knowing that this will be something special, since they each had to agree that if they were to come to the party, they would wear a pair of my satin panties under their casual, street clothes.

This party is different. I staged my little party so there would be three sound proof rooms on the second floor of my loft. Each room door was numbered 1, 2 and 3. As my guests were arriving and drawing numbers to determine who they would be partnered with for the evening, I could see looks of puzzlement creep over their faces.

All my guests wore regular street clothes, except Martha. There is something different about Martha. She looks like she had just awakened from a long winter's nap…so fresh and healthy and very, very sexy. Maybe it is that sheer, light blue, skirt that she is wearing or maybe it was the white blouse or was it her hair? Whatever it is, she looks stunning and sexy at the same time.

I could not figure it out, until I realized this is the "new Martha." She has been taking Yoga classes, working out, and consciously working on herself with a life coach who specializes in finding the *you*, you want to be. I feel envious of her, how comfortable and confident she looks!

Oh well, after having John, Dr. Larson and Mr. Peterson arrive early at staggered times and giving each just enough Valium to calm them down but not enough to make them sleepy, I put each one of them alone in one of the rooms behind the numbered doors, one, two and three.

After the guests arrived, the frivolous behavior, including partaking of wine and couple foreplay, began spontaneously. Soon it was time for my evenings' announcement and I step onto my little stage in front of the doors.

"Quiet, quiet," I say loudly, followed by a little shshs-ing help from some of my quests, and couple more calls for quiet from those with control issues—just a bit of a chore to get their attention at this point.

"Thank you," and then I announce to the group, "We have three special guests tonight and one of them is behind each door. One, Two, and Three."

Hoots. Cat calls. Some wondering why they weren't behind the doors.

When things were quieted down again, I ask the group, "All right, who do you want to meet first, the guest behind door number one, door number two or door number three? I think to myself that this must be how Monty Hall felt when he asked this question on his show, Let's Make a Deal.

A momentary brief silence follows my announcement, as if the group were thinking really hard about this decision. This group thinking, imagine that!

"Open Door Number Three!" shouts a group in the back corner. Ever so slowly I dramatically open door three and out walks Mr. Peterson in a different way that I had ever seen him walk before. When he sees the naked or half-naked bodies lying around, he just smiles and begins to remove his clothing, until he comes to my panties which have an extremely large bulge in the front. Before I realize it, he is masturbating to the cheers of the crowd. Everyone knows the kind of panties I wear because they have all seen them before, and most have worn them.

A man calls out, "Harder, harder!" At that point Mr. Peterson tears off my satin panties and jumps into the crowd to have fun. He never realized that his wife, Joan, has always been a part of our "networking" group. To his delight, Joan is right in front, cheering him on because her husband had finally began to realize what fun sex is. After an entangled embrace, Joan leads him to one of the pillows nests, where they lie down and continue. It takes several minutes for things to quiet back down again.

"All right, it is time to pick another door." I announce.

This time it is unanimous, as they shout together, "Door number two."

I opened the door, and there was Dr. Larson who said, "Begin." as he stepped out of his door. There was dead silence, and then he began taking off his clothes like a stripper, stripping and humming to himself and twirling his shirt above his head to the soft music that I had programmed into the audio system that filled one side of the room. When Dr. Larson got to my panties, he stopped, stopped dead—no movement at all. Then he slowly called out, "Martha, come up here."

The new sexy Martha jumped up on our little stage and began tearing her clothes off, as he assisted her, throwing them out into the now half-drunken crowd, while with his other hand, Dr Larson began to rub his penis through my panties. Then he threw them off, and he and Martha had intercourse right there on the hard little stage to the cheers of the crowd.

When they were done they just collapsed in sleep on a corner of the carpeted, small stage. This annoyed some of the group, but I shrugged and stepped over the Larsons, letting they enjoy a much deserved sleep.

Without asking the group, I simply walked to door number one, quietly opening it. John peacefully and quietly approached me. No wet spots showed on his pants. He faintly smiled at the group of partiers and with a big smile extended his hand to me. What a shock!

"Hold my hand," he asked, while he with his other hand started to remove his clothing. It was a graceless, stumbling act, while holding tightly to my hand.

When he got to his panties, he smiled and said gently and softly, "You will be proud of me," and then he played with his penis until the bigness was obvious and that bigness released a joyful great puddle of semen on the floor. As the crowd cheered, he took my hand, gently and quietly said, "Thank you!" and returned, after letting go of my hand, back behind door one, closing it ever so gently.

Some of the crowd was drunk by now, and some had left, and some were asleep, but I felt a strange tingling in my soul. The happy tingling was one that I could not identify so I went to sleep on the floor with the rest of the group.

I woke at around eight the next morning. Mr. Peterson and his wife and Dr. Larson and Martha had left during the night, but John was still a sleep behind door number one.

As I gently kicked the sleeping drunks to wake them up, most of them began leaving in someone else's clothes, but they all left groggy-eyed and happy.

There were a couple comments that I should serve breakfast with Bloody Marys, too. Then John came out of door one, leaned down, giving me a gentle, loving kiss on my right cheek, and left. How could he kiss my cheek and be loving when I was such a mess? After sleeping all night, I looked rumpled, hair messed up, blouse wrinkled and my make up was a mess, but as always I had not had sex with anyone that night.

The morning after is always clean-up time, but no worry, because Jan-King, my usual cleaning crew, always arrives at 9:30 a.m. sharp, and things always look better than they did before the party began by noon. They even take down the little stage and props we use, but I store away the mat that John had slept on myself.

Locked in my master suite, I take a warm but not hot bath, have two Bloody Mary's and felt the same happy tingling that I had felt the night before. Then it comes to me, as if in a big spurt of semen, John, gentle, kind John. It is John.

Post Script

My real name is Susan DeJung, MD. I am an internationally-known, Certified Sex Therapist. I help people with their sexual problems for money. I charge five thousand dollars per session, plus expenses. Thus, Mrs. Peterson, Dr Larson and John's fraternity alumni paid me lots of money to help them. I figured that I had made about sixty thousand having sex therapy with just these three professionals. I do this in addition to my design business, and I have become quite comfortable financially.

Finally, John and I were married two months after his coming out party. The alums were willing to pay me because they saw his potential as a truly brilliant psychologist. After our marriage, the parties stopped and so did my sex therapy surrogate work. Escabelle moved on to the West Coast and hasn't called in a couple years. John is so gentle and kind, and he is such a great psychologist, really making an international name for himself.

Now I am wealthy in so many ways.

The end. The real end!

Or is it the real beginning?

About the Author

You have now visited the secret world of psychotherapeutic trysts.